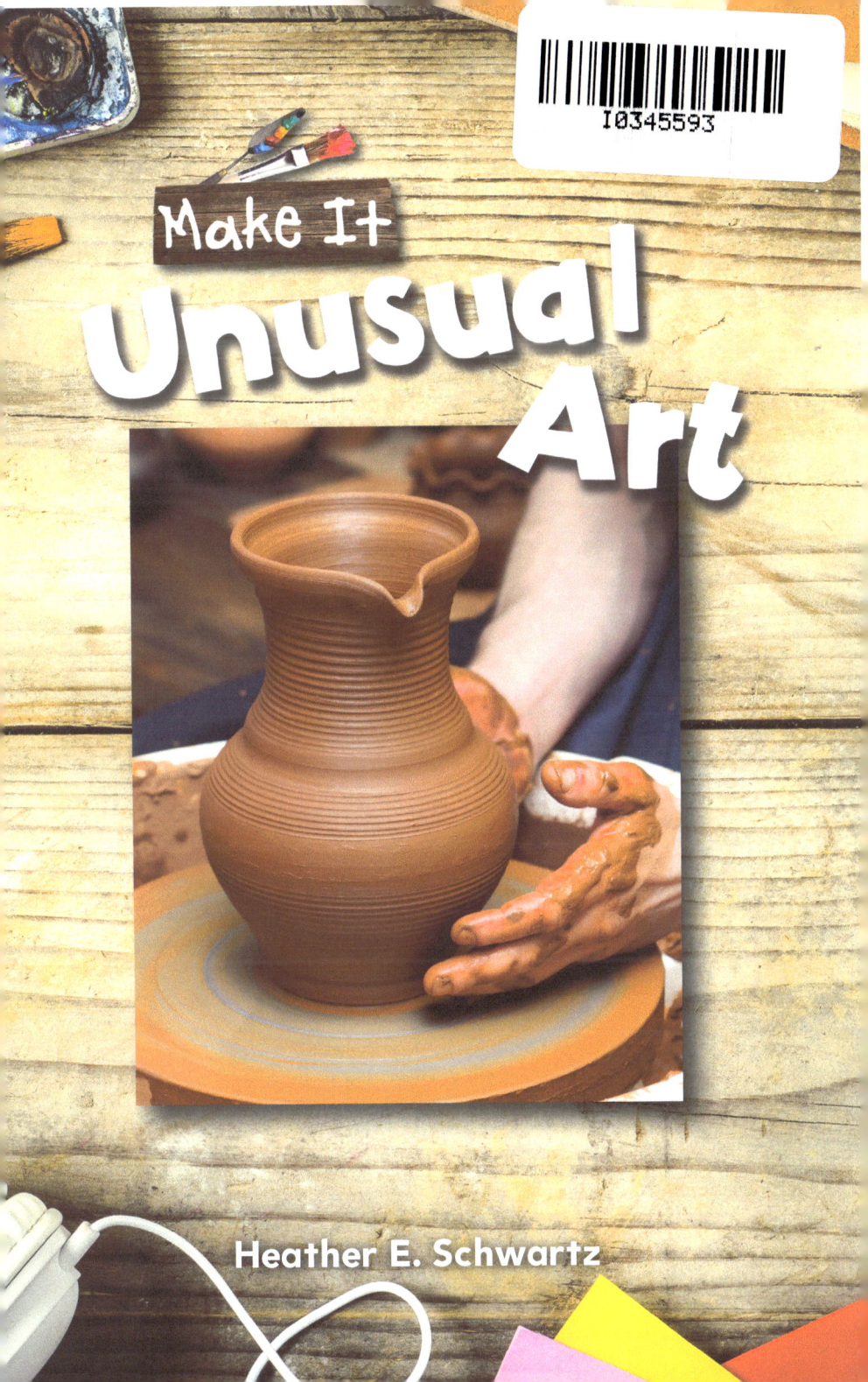

Make It
Unusual Art

Heather E. Schwartz

Publishing Credits

Rachelle Cracchiolo, M.S.Ed., *Publisher*
Conni Medina, M.A.Ed., *Managing Editor*
Nika Fabienke, Ed.D., *Series Developer*
June Kikuchi, *Content Director*
John Leach, *Assistant Editor*
Kevin Pham, *Graphic Designer*

TIME For Kids and the TIME For Kids logo are registered trademarks of TIME Inc. Used under license.

Image Credits: p.8 View Apart/Shutterstock.com; p.13 PhotonCatcher/Shutterstock.com; all other images from iStock and/or Shutterstock.

Library of Congress Cataloging-in-Publication Data

Names: Schwartz, Heather E., author.
Title: Make it : unusual art / Heather E. Schwartz.
Description: Huntington Beach, CA : Teacher Created Materials, 2018. | Audience: K to Grade 3.
Identifiers: LCCN 2017026884 (print) | LCCN 2017027509 (ebook) | ISBN 9781425853327 (eBook) | ISBN 9781425849580 (pbk.)
Subjects: LCSH: Art--Technique--Juvenile literature.
Classification: LCC N7433 (ebook) | LCC N7433 .S39 2018 (print) | DDC 701/.8--dc23
LC record available at https://lccn.loc.gov/2017026884

Teacher Created Materials

5301 Oceanus Drive
Huntington Beach, CA 92649-1030
http://www.tcmpub.com

ISBN 978-1-4258-4958-0

© 2018 Teacher Created Materials, Inc.

Artists turn ideas into art.
How do they do it?
They might use paint, **clay**, or metal.
They might use wood, sand, and food.

Artists work with paint.
They choose colors and a blank **canvas**.
A canvas can be square or round.
Some look like rectangles.

Artists work with clay.
They use their hands and other tools to mold it into shapes.
They create **sculptures** and dishes.

Artists work with metal.
They create sculptures.
Some look like real objects.
Others do not.

Artists work with wood.
They carve wood.
They cut wood into shapes.
They can use wood to make tables and chairs.

Artists work with sand.
They move it into shapes
and **patterns**.
Sand art washes away
with the tide.

Artists even work with food.
They change how it looks.
They make sculptures.
They make food art.

You can make food art.
Get a strong paper plate
and white glue.
Get all kinds of dry **pasta**.

Put pasta on the flat part of the plate. Choose different shapes and sizes. Add colors and make a pattern.
Make a picture.

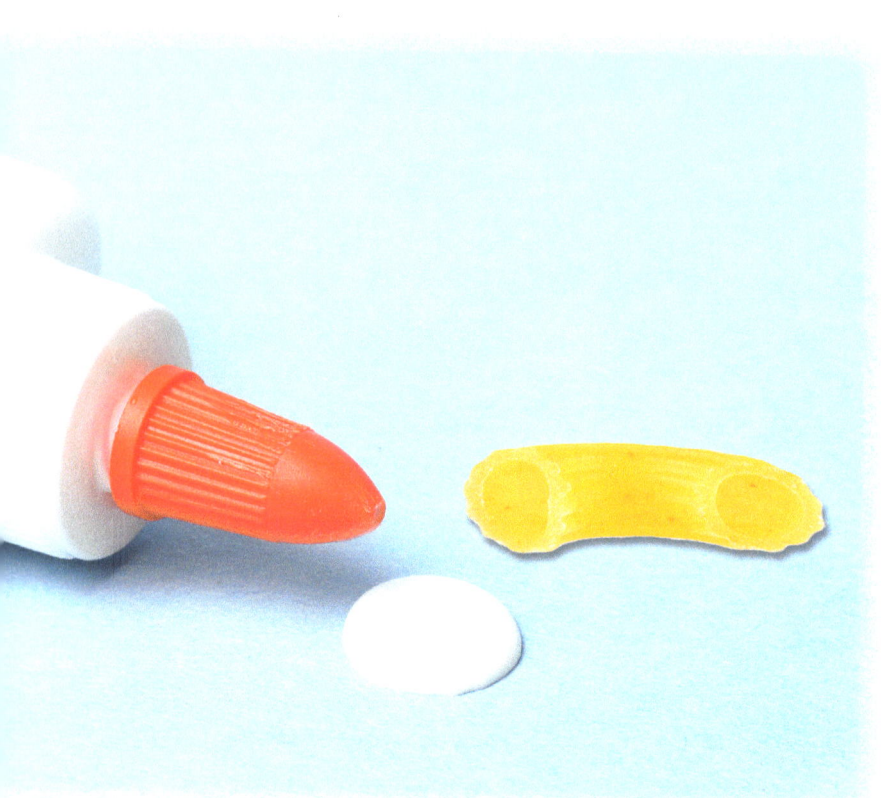

Glue each piece of pasta into place.
Let it dry.
Your artwork is done!

Artists use all kinds of materials to make art. You can make art, too. You can be an artist.

Glossary

canvas

clay

pasta

patterns

sculptures

www.ingramcontent.com/pod-product-compliance
Lightning Source LLC
Chambersburg PA
CBHW042059290426
44113CB00001B/19